I Do, Do You?

Advice from God for Marital Success

By Chris J. Schimel

No Celebrity Endorsements Here

I haven't asked well known authors or celebrities to write endorsements for ***I Do, Do You? Instead, I have asked couples that have read it and benefited from it to give you their impressions.*** This mini-book has been in manuscript form for several years and I have given it to people whose marriages I thought could benefit from it, and pre-marital couples before their weddings. Here is what a few had to say about ***I Do, Do You?***

"*I Do, Do You?* was a great read! It really helped us to lay a foundation for the start of our marriage. If you are deciding to take the next step in your relationship we highly recommend this book."

—Jeremy and Kaytie Savaet
(Twenty-Something Newlyweds)

"*I Do, Do You?* is based solely on biblical principles and addresses multiple thought-provoking points often overlooked but paramount in a marital relationship. It addresses a balance of issues for both sexes and is uniquely profound in its content, yet easy to read and apply. We highly recommend this mini-book to any couple wanting to lay a solid foundation for a lasting relationship."

—Tom & Julie LaPorte
(Fifty-Something Remarried Divorcees)

"*I Do, Do You?* was inspirational. It reminds us to be more aware of what we need to do in our marriage. We would recommend this book without reservation to anyone!"

—Steve and Jen Montella
(Forty-Something Newlyweds)

Other books by Chris Schimel

Touch One

Beautiful Behaviors

Once Broken

Murder in the Church

Lessons of the Fall
*E-Book
See Chris' website

A Story of Rage
*E-Book
See Chris' website

Between You and Me
Mini E-Book
See Chris' website

Ripples
Mini E-Book
See Chris' website

*Soon to be hard
copy also

Copyright © 2020 By Chris J. Schimel
All rights reserved.

ISBN Paperback: 978-1-64746-103-4
ISBN Hardback: 978-1-64746-104-1
ISBN Ebook: 978-1-64746-105-8
Library of Congress Control Number: 2020900113

Some Scripture quotations are from the New King James Version of the Bible. Copyright © 1979, 1980, 1982 by Thomas Nelson, Inc., publishers. Used by permission.

Unless otherwise noted, Scripture quotations are taken from the Holy Bible, New Living Translation, Copyright © 1996, 2004, 2007 by Tyndale House Foundation. Used by permission of Tyndale House Publishers, Inc., Carol Stream, Illinois 60188. All rights reserved.

I Do, Do You?...
is a book that takes its authority
from God's Word, mostly
from Ephesians 5:21-31, where under
the inspiration of the Holy Spirit
Paul instructs how husbands and wives
are to live and love each other
the most effectively
to make their marriages work
the most successfully.

DEDICATION

This book is dedicated to the one I love:
Shirley, my wife, partner in ministry and
life-long best friend.
Together we have employed these principles and
have experienced
all God intended marriage to be.

Contents

1 The Basis for Marital Success 1

2 Women 7
- Selfless
- Equal
- Reasonableness
- Lean

3 Men 23
- One - Sacrifice
- Two - Conversation
- Three - Intimacy
- Four - The Golden Rule of Marriage
- Five - Triple Spirituality

4 Mutual Submission. 43
- Listen
- Release
- Forgiveness
- I'm Sorry
- Rightness
- Exclamation Point!

5 Questions for Study –
Building Marital DNA 57

"I Do. Do You?" Is a book diagnosing one of the causes for the tragedy
in the true story of **Chris Schimel's** book . . .

"Murder in the Church"

The Most Important **Introduction** You'll Ever Read.

Don't skip it!

I Do, Do You? is the little sister of the book that tells my shocking true story titled *Murder in the Church*. In *Murder in the Church* marital coldness was the primary seed that sprouted the tragedy in its pages. Similar tragedies, perhaps less shocking but equally tragic, are incubating in countless marriages across our globe. However, if the premises in this tiny book are applied and practiced, they will warm cooling relationships and keep the fires burning in marriages that are just getting ignited.

Most marriages begin with naïve, inaccurate assumptions and fanciful ideas in both men and women about what marriage success involves. Brides are blinded by love and fantasy, and the media is no help. It continues to communicate that marriages are all about the feelings of love, soul mates, true love and the like. Grooms, well, generally speaking, they are just blind, but not because they are aloof. They are blind because they feel landing the woman they targeted is a sign insuring future success. They've won their bride. They've conquered. All should be fine.

Don't get me wrong, there are very real feelings of love for each other in both men and women. However, once those emotions fade; (and they will fade) everything changes. Most brides and grooms on their wedding day are clueless as to those changes. They are clueless because their feelings of love suggest that they will feel this way about each other forever.

No newlywed suspects that his or her marriage will be battling coldness in a few short years or less.

The larger percentage of marriages begin with such mythical assumptions as…*our marriage will be different, we have love;* or, *landing a spouse is an omen for future happiness;* or as I said above, *the way we feel now is the way we will always feel.* And the famous Christian myth; *we are Christians. We believe marriage is forever so, it will be.*

To be more accurate, love doesn't fade. But in time the initial feelings that come with *finding love* do fade and evolve into a different kind of love, a love that is less about feelings and more about actions. And as the actions are lived out a second level of love, more like adoration appears.

I heard once that when people experience the phenomenon of falling in love, a chemical is secreted in the body that enhances those feelings. If you have ever fallen in love, you may indeed believe this to be true. Those feelings seem almost magical, and yet real, but are also powerful. However, within two to three years after couples first experience these feelings, the chemical secretion ceases. At least that's the theory. It is then that a baton is passed to the next level of love in a relationship which involves actions that produce adoration. However, if the actions aren't done, adoration doesn't happen either. Instead a cold war breaks out.

Actually, marriage is kind of a trap; in that, there is an allurement that is couched in the emotions of finding love. Couples are, in a way, baited and lured into marriage. And the funny part is…it is God who is doing the luring. Why would He do that?

Well, He doesn't do it with each individual relationship. He does it by the way He has made men and women which has to do with the age-old testosterone versus estrogen factor, and the drive and need in humans for sexual companionship. These are the allurements.

Here are the reasons He does this.

First, He does it because when marriage is done His way, there is great fulfillment and happiness for married couples—happiness He wants for them. So, He isn't really luring us to our deaths, as a trapper would lure an animal to the kill. Instead, He is luring us to a potential for fullness in life.

Second, He knows as we work through the issues of matrimony, relying on Him to guide us, we will become more conformed to the image of Christ (Romans 8:29). He alone knows there is no more important and no more life-giving objective for humans than to become increasingly conformed into the likeness of Jesus. Marriage is probably the best refining environment for this purpose, and the parenthood it usually generates is the second.

Since the emotions that accompany finding love fade, successful marriages have learned what to do when the initial feelings of love diminish.

I Do, Do You? is written from the standpoint that scriptural instruction about marriage fully understands this shift from the emotions of finding love to the adoration of acting love out. This is apparent in the language scripture uses in its instruction about marriage.

All parts of this book should be read by both the man and the woman. However, when answering the questions in the back, some parts are for the woman to answer, and some are for the man. But it wouldn't be a bad idea for both to know what questions are being asked of the other.

To conclude this introduction, I would like to clarify the "God-advice" suggestion in the sub-title of this book. The Bible is God's Word. That means He wrote it. 1 Timothy 3:16 tells us that all scripture, though penned by human authors, is written by God.

All of the principles in *I Do, Do You?* are gleaned from God's Word. Most come from Ephesians 5:21-31, the premier passage in the Bible about marriage, but others are addressed. The Ephesians verses will be listed at a certain point. These principles involves my perspective, but they are sound scriptural concepts that contain golden nuggets of truth that if followed will fan the early flames of love, rekindle otherwise cooling marriages, as well as rescue frigid unions on the verge of being frozen forever.

> *"'Your words' are more desirable than gold, even the finest gold. They are sweeter than honey, even honey dripping from the comb. They are a warning to your servant, a great reward for those who obey them."*
> Psalms 19:10-11 (NLT)

This is a HUGE little book on marriage.

1

The Basis for Marital Success

If I asked you to describe the perfect woman and the perfect man, I know exactly what you would say.

The *perfect woman* is five foot four, with a thin waste, a perfect figure, a beautiful face, a flawless complexion, shapely legs and long flowing hair.

The *perfect man* is robust, six foot tall, a handsome face, with six pack abs, bulging muscles, a full head of hair and a strong chin.

How about it? Was I right; or at least close?

Take Adam and Eve. When we think of the first couple, we don't think of them as being overweight, with scraggly hair, pitted faces, big noses, short stubby legs and scabby knees—do we? My guess is, most of us would think of them as being perfect tens.

There was a lady in one of the churches I pastored who was convinced that both Adam and Jesus must have been the most perfect, handsome and attractive men to have ever lived. And no one could convince her otherwise.

She felt this about Adam because he was the first man and if he started out bad it would have just gotten worse from there and would have resulted in the whole human race being ugly. That hasn't happened so he must have been a real hunk, and she felt the same way about Eve. That was her reasoning.

She felt that Jesus had to have been at least as handsome as Adam, probably more-so, because He was God's Son and how could God have made his own Son ugly. That also, was her reasoning. It is clear that she attributed great value to physical attractiveness.

I would call her thinking somewhat strange, except, in many of the pictures we see of Jesus, artists throughout history seem to have the same opinion. Even in all of the modern Jesus movies we see today, it looks like the directors found the best looking guys they could find to play the part. In all of their renditions of the Savior, He looks a lot like the sexiest man alive.

Actually, I don't know about Adam, but the scripture says Jesus wasn't at all attractive (Isaiah 53:2). It says there, *"He had no form or comeliness and when we saw Him there was no beauty that we should desire Him."* When you stop and think about it, it makes perfect sense. Wouldn't it be just like God to not just make Jesus a common person born in a stable, but also make Him a little unattractive? I mean, think about it. We have enough trouble trying to get people to follow Jesus for the right reasons without Him being a gorgeous guy.

God's idea of the perfect man and woman is much different than ours. In this book I don't want to describe that for you in so many words; but by the time we are finished I hope you will have a better idea of what both Adam and Eve might have looked like—I mean, martially and spiritually speaking; and what the perfect man and woman in marriage should look like.

So let's begin with the first couple. After all, concerning marriage, they were the ones who got the ball rolling.

As soon as God appeared in the garden that first day of Adam and Eve's sin, He made a gruesome discovery. His perfect creation of a man, and His perfect creation of a woman, had become grotesque. Now, outwardly, they still looked like the perfect man and woman He first made. But God has the ability to see below the surface of things. And, as He peered into their souls they looked deformed, disfigured, ugly and hideous.

God said to the woman, "Your lot will be sorrow, pain and subservience." Genesis 3:16 reads, "I will greatly multiply your sorrow and your conception; in pain will you bring forth children; *your desire will be for your husband, and he shall rule over you.*" (NKJV)

Most don't realize the basis for all marital issues between the sexes is contained in the last thirteen words of this verse, "*your desire shall be for your husband, and he shall rule over you.*"

These words tell us that before the fall men and women were equal. There was no domineering. There was no unequal treatment. Eve wasn't trampled on by her husband, or abused, or controlled, or talked down to in any way. She wasn't exploited by him, or treated as the little woman, or the baby machine, or the kitchen slave, or the whipping post. The fall produced all of those treatments.

But there was something about the way God made her from her husband's side, and how sin and a subsequent loss of self-esteem and connection with God interacted with their relationship, that caused massive confusion with how men would relate to women—and how women would relate to men. And our world has been trying to figure out how to relate to the opposite sex ever since.

Not long ago my wife and I had a little spat. I was trying to figure out her reasoning for why she spoke and felt the way she did about whatever it was that we were bickering about. But I couldn't for the life of me make sense out of it, or her, or women in general. Then I realized I wasn't supposed to make sense out of it. It's part of the curse. I am just supposed to say "I'm sorry" and go away more confused than ever. I am just glad that at the moment of my apology she didn't ask me what I was sorry for because I didn't have a clue. I just knew I'd better be sorry.

Well, unfortunately; the issues concerning the sexes are much more serious than a little spat between spouses. They aren't issues between—they are issues that proceed from within. Let's begin by looking at the premiere scripture in the Bible about marriage.

> *"And further, submit to one another out of reverence for Christ. For wives, this means submit to your husbands as to the Lord. For a husband is the head of his wife as Christ is the head of the church. He is the Savior of his body, the church. As the church submits to Christ, so you wives should submit to your husbands in everything. For husbands, this means love your wives, just as Christ loved the church. He*

The Basis For Marital Success

gave up his life for her to make her holy and clean, washed by the cleansing of God's Word. He did this to present her to himself as a glorious church without a spot or wrinkle or any other blemish. Instead, she will be holy and without fault. In the same way, husbands ought to love their wives as they love their own bodies. For a man who loves his wife actually shows love for himself. No one hates his own body but feeds and cares for it, just as Christ cares for the church. And we are members of his body. As the Scriptures say, 'A man leaves his father and mother and is joined to his wife, and the two are united into one.'"

Ephesians 5:21-31(NLT)

2

Women

As we attempt to understand these "issues within", let's begin by talking about the female component of marriage. I see four key issues addressed directly or indirectly in this scripture to married ladies.

> *"For wives, this means submit to your husbands as to the Lord. For a husband is the head of his wife as Christ is the head of the church. He is the Savior of his body, the church. As the church submits to Christ, so you wives should submit to your husbands in everything."*
>
> Ephesians 5:22-24 (NLT)

Selfless

God made women with an incredible amount of *selfless love* for their families. This is suggested in the scripture above when it introduces the idea of submission. Submission is not a restriction, as so many believe; it is a character-ability that understands human nature—both men and women. God instructs women in this way because He knows only a woman can do it and it is a result of the way God made the human female; and one benefit of this design is selflessness. One can only imagine how much selfless love women would have possessed had humans not fallen. I'll talk more about submission later.

When forest fire fighters surveyed the aftermath of the infamous Storm King Mountain Fire that took place near Glenwood Springs, Colorado in July of 1994, they were taken aback by the devastation. The fire hadn't just destroyed acres of forest, it killed fourteen fire fighters.

While investigating the destruction, one man saw a bird up against the base of a tree that was standing with its wings spread down around itself. It had been crystalized by the extreme heat. It looked so bizarre the man nudged it with his boot. When he did it crumbled and out from under the dead mother scurried three little chicks. This mother bird had gathered her three babies under her wings and had protected them from the fire's heat without consideration of her own life, and did so until the very moment life slipped out of her body.

That is exactly the way my wife is with her children and family.

She is a remarkable specimen of a human being. She works tirelessly for her family even when she is exhausted. She is an outstanding cook. She has never failed even one day in all of her almost 50 years of family oversight to have an exceptional and creative meal on the table for her family. She has a job as a counselor, putting more than twenty hours a week into it. She put's at least 25 hours into the church we serve each week working on the computer, graphic designs, worship, teaching and other projects for no renumeration. She honors her extended family with regular phone calls or visits and keeps a home inside and out in impeccable fashion. And I could go on.

Proverbs 31 describes the perfect woman and looks almost impossible to duplicate. But after observing my wife, and not just her, but many other women I have known over the years; I have to say these miracles do exist. I have never met a man with this kind of sacrificial and selfless devotion to his family.

There are some obvious reasons for this.

First, all women have mothering instincts. It's why most little girls have a doll of some sort with them most everywhere they go.

Every time little nine-year-old Allie sees two-year-old Ellie in our church, she immediately goes into mother-mode. She hugs her, holds her hand, tries to pick her up, helps her walk up the stairs and in short, takes on the mother-role, because God has placed in all females mothering instincts.

Second, mothers facilitate the conception of their children and carry their babies in their own bodies for nine months. In no uncertain terms their children are part of them. Fathers can't quite feel the same emotions and inner connections as birthing mothers do.

Third, part of the "help-meet or helper" (Genesis 2:18) designation and blueprint God used to design and assemble his human female creation, reflects this selflessness in women.

In our world today there is a trend for women to break out of the stereotypes of the past and become entrepreneurs, business executives, CEO's, Kung Fu experts and super heroes. I am all for the emergence of women in our society. I even believe it is prophesied in the Bible (Joel 2:28-29) and is part of God's plan for women and for our world.

However, my advice to ladies is: in your efforts to follow the trends for women today, don't give them all to the workplace and have nothing left for home. These qualities identify what a woman is and are necessary qualities for a marriage and family to succeed.

These qualities not only define who He made women to be, they are what have made women desirable and effective in entrepreneurship and corporate industry. They are the qualities that the world would like to see emerge in business. They are who you are. If women were to abandon them in family interactions, it would be disastrous for our families and our world. And, some of what women are doing today to pursue careers and female emergence are requiring their selfless love for their families to be compromised.

Men need for you to live these qualities out in the lives of the people in your families. Don't just *follow* the drives in you to have a husband and a family. Ladies, you are drawn to romantic love and to have a family because it is a drive God has placed in you. But if the selfless love he has made in you, along with the mothering instincts and helper qualities he has also endowed you with, get placed on the back burner in favor of changing the world, your families and the families of our world will be in serious trouble. Follow also the drives in you to make your families the loving families God intended when he made you the way He did.

So, what's a woman to do?

I think she should ask God to help her to be the best *self-less* lover to her husband and family she can be. She is wired that way anyway. She might as well be the best image of herself possible.

As stated above, Proverbs 31 describes this person in detail. It is a very biblical goal and potential objective for women because it is the way He has made them. Ladies shouldn't think it is an impossible task. When my wife was younger she used to think it was an unreachable goal; and she did not, nor could she, measure up. But the more she faithfully served the Lord, and the more she was devoted to the roles of wife and motherhood, the closer she got to the selfless woman in Proverbs 31.

Truly, women are capable of being less than this. But women are the best model of God's self-sacrificing love that exists in the world. And men need a model to follow, one they can see.

Jesus, of course, was the greatest selfless lover of all and His model was certainly outstanding as He died for all mankind on a cross of torture. But men need a visual. With Jesus historical example to men of this from the cross, and a wife's example living it out before him every day so he can see how it works, in time a husband will get it. It may take some men the greater part of a lifetime to get it. But most will.

So, wives; don't become weary in well-doing (Galatians 6:9). We husbands are pretty thick headed. It takes some time for us to catch on. In fact, selfless love could be defined as loving, even while others aren't getting it. It's why they call it selfless love. Please ladies, be the unique selfless humans God created you to be. Don't go so far that you feel walked on or used, and don't get frustrated with us when we are so self-focused we are out in left field somewhere and not catching on. Just love us anyway and in time we will get it, and we may even notice and commend you for how selflessly you love.

And please ladies, don't give all your selflessness to your careers, because if you do it will shortchange your family—your marriage included. This quality was designed in you first and foremost for your husband and children. Your business and your bosses love it at work. But it really wasn't intended for the corporate world. It was intended for your marriages and families. It is ok to give to a point, but don't forget why you were given the quality in the first place.

Equal

Next, God made men and women *equal*.

I am somewhat ashamed that there are some Christians who have taken the scriptures to mean that women are lesser because of the way Eve was tempted to sin, and therefore should be treated lesser (1 Peter 2:11-15). Some even take Peter's reference to women being the "weaker vessel" (1 Peter 3:7) to mean that they are "lesser vessels." And the laugher about this is; these men actually think they are superior morally to their women. None of it is true.

It is the women who attend church. It is the women who do ministry. It is the women who are unafraid to worship the Lord. It is the women who see to it that their children attend church. And it is the women who pray their husbands, not only into the church, but into the kingdom of God. My feeling is that without women in our churches most would close their doors for a lack of interest. You can't convince me that men are superior spiritually. Men and women were created equal, and are still equal—different but equal.

God made men and women equal, but when mankind sinned we didn't lose that equality. We only lost the ability to treat each other as equals. That is why women are abused. Men's lack of self-esteem abuses; women's lack of self-esteem accepts it.

The oppression women experience from domination by men is a result of sin, not a punishment for sin. The reason I say this is because most of the mental, physical, emotional and sexual domination and mistreatment men exact on women is sinful and an abomination before God.

Would a holy God be saying in Genesis 3:16, "Woman, you've sinned and I am going to sanction your husband's sinful, violent, and abusive treatment upon you as the punishment you deserve? His abuse of you is accomplishing my bidding of chastisement." If I understand the scriptures correctly; this could never be God's intention or plan.

But women do need to remember, and some may need to be convinced, that they are equal to their men—not superior. I say this because along with the trend for women to emerge from old patterns and change past stereotypes, there also seems to be a feeling in women that they should rise above men and dominate them.

I'm sure the media has encouraged this mindset. But it will only be an improvement in our world if women emerge to equality and don't aspire to reach for superiority over men. That will offset the balance in another way.

Men and women were always equal. Sin kept their equality hidden. If women try to aspire beyond God's original design, our world will be in trouble in a whole new way.

So what's a woman to do?

My advice to women is: be content in your 21st Century emergence to be equal, both in your accomplishments and in your thinking. Don't aspire to dominate, either in your new place in society or in your marriage. Seek to find equal ground to stand together—not apart, level with your husband, not above him. It is part of what 'submit to one another' in verse 21 means.

Be the *equal* but different being God created you to be. Men can think their jobs, their strength, and their greater inclination toward logic, versus the female tendency toward emotions, makes them superior. But it doesn't. It only makes them different.

Don't let the voices of our culture and its male-influence persuade you to digress to feeling inferior. You are complimentary to the traits of maleness not inferior to them. If you cave to the cultural norm, imbalance will result; as it has throughout the history of the world, and the outcome will be abuse. That doesn't mean you should fight for equality. History has proven that doesn't work either.

How do women remain equal? By being confident in the way God made you enough to be the equal person you were designed to be. The modern trend for women in our culture is to act, or even be, superior to men. But that doesn't work either. It just causes more strife. Just be confident that you are equal.

Demonstrate the emotions you feel with wisdom, because as you do, it will help your husband reach his emotional potential. That will help him find balance in his treatment of his wife. And don't let him off the hook when he doesn't feel like talking because he needs to talk even if he doesn't feel like it. Maybe he doesn't need as much conversation as you do but he needs far more than he thinks he does and talking will help him sort out his perceptions. Be confident in your equality so you can lead your husband into feeling what you know, and God knows he needs to feel. It will set him free and cause him to be the husband and man God made him to be. You are more emotionally sensitive than your husband. But that doesn't mean he has no emotion. He does. Remember, you are equal. You both are emotional creatures.

Too many women allow the inferior feelings our culture, males in general, and sometimes their own husbands try to impose on them; to cause them to feel inferior and act inferior. If the modern trend is for women to try to act superior, it only confirms that the ancient age-old way for women has been to act inferior. But both superiority and inferiority are lies. No one, male or female, is inferior which means no one is superior. For a woman to feel either toward a man is to believe a lie. So ladies, be the equal person you are. Your husband and family desperately need for you to do that.

> *"In the same way, you husbands must give honor to your wives. Treat your wife with understanding as you live together. She may be weaker than you are, but she is your equal partner in God's gift of new life. Treat her as you should so your prayers will not be hindered."*
>
> I Peter 3:7 (NLT)

Reasonableness

It seems to me that women in general usually have the greatest amount of *reasonableness* when it comes to marital conflict, concerns and decision making. If there are ten wacky ideas or inappropriate ways of thinking or behaving concerning how marriage should work, women will have three of the ten and men will have the other seven; and vice-versa, women will have seven of the rational ideas and men will have three.

As a man I would like to be able to say trouble in marriage is a 50-50 proposition—that the cause of issues between the sexes is at least half and half. But it's my experience that it is not. However, the reason isn't because men are less reasonable. It is because the buck stops with men and they have refused to take up the challenge.

Furthermore, it has been proposed that men are thinkers and women are feelers, and I don't necessarily disagree with this. In addition they say, men are better at math and women are better at English. This is easily proven by research and statistics. The problem lies in how we interpret this from a value perspective. Unfortunately, both educated and uneducated people interpret these discoveries in a way that ascribes worth and value—or the lack thereof.

Men will tend to translate the thinker/feeler-math/English comparison to mean that men think through things and therefore reason things more effectively. While women just decide with more haphazard emotionally unmeasurable and uncertain methodologies because men *are* thinkers and women *are* feelers; and thinking is better than feeling. But none of this interpretation is true. Women think plenty and because men don't feel very effectively, they miss a lot of the reasonableness their wives can provide.

There are great amounts of reasonableness in the feelings of women.

For example: A couple may have a contractor in their living room talking to them about a proposal he is making to put an addition onto their home. The husband may like the numbers and the timeline and the extras the contractor promised and he may conclude; it all sounds good.

However, the wife may say, "I don't feel good about him." When the husband asks why, she may respond, "I don't know, I just don't feel comfortable with this guy."

Men at this point may be tempted to think…*there's that feeling thing again. There is nothing solid to make a decision on. I think this is the guy.*

However, if he was to press his wife further and ask her to explain why she didn't feel good about the man, she would perhaps, be able to explain some very reasonable and yet undetected observations by her husband.

She might say, "I didn't like the way he hesitated when you asked him about the time line. And, I heard him contradict himself three times about things he said earlier. And I didn't like his insensitivity to our daughter's illness."

The husband didn't even notice these things. He couldn't feel them, but she could. And her feelings were very influenced by reason and cognition. They were just triggered by feelings that only a woman can sense.

When considering a woman's mind from this perspective, they are very reasonable and very necessary when considering decision-making in a family.

My advice to women is: don't let self-esteem, shyness, ignorance or intimidation cause you to shrink back from sharing this perspective of reasonableness in your marriage and in every aspect of your home and family. Your husband needs it desperately. He may not know how to extract it from you, and he may be threatened by some of it. But he needs it. And, as much as it has been called emotionally uncertain and not based in reason, it is nothing of the kind. It is reason from another vantage point that men aren't able to see.

So what's a woman to do?

Ladies, use the *reasonableness* you possess to help bring balance to the choices your husbands and families make. The ability to feel can be translated "intuition", which can translate into wisdom, and then into common sense and then into reasonableness. It's a gut feeling.

I don't know how many times my wife has told me something like...*I'm not sure I feel right about this decision.* What was she saying? She was saying it didn't make sense to her. Her gut was saying no. That is reason. Those reasonable suggestions have gotten us out of a lot of messes. And here, it's men who think they are the ones with all the common sense!

Lean

I want to address just one more concern...and it's that submission thing that Ephesians 5:22-24 addresses and our protesting culture, especially women, keep resisting as oppressive.

> *"Wives, submit to your own husbands, as to the Lord. For the husband is head of the wife, as also Christ is head of the church; and He is the Savior of the body. Therefore, just as the church is subject to Christ, so let the wives be to their own husbands in everything."*
> Ephesians 5:22-24 (NKJV)

"In everything" doesn't refer to all things without question regardless of what he asks of her moral or immoral, smart or ignorant, foolish or wise. It refers to another term I will be explaining more fully later in this book. It refers to a heart that has a fully submitted attitude of respect to the man she is married to.

However, the word "submit" doesn't just ruffle the feathers of most women today. It evokes violent reactions, especially in our feministic culture—and even among some Christian women. But I would like for you to consider a different interpretation than the word submit. I'm not opposed to the word. I just think it has been tainted with cultural misunderstanding.

First, as I mentioned earlier, submission is not a restriction; it is a character-ability that understands the nature of both men and women. It is a quality that must exist in marriage. Without it marriages are doomed to fail. This section of scripture begins with and states (verse 21) that submission is mutual for both men and women and calls for the quality to be present in both husbands and wives. I deal with this more extensively in the last chapter of this book. Submission was never intended to be a dominant/subordinate suggestion. It is a <u>mutually</u> necessary quality that should be present in both marriage parties. However, the suggestion that women should submit to their husbands in the next few verses has been met with great resistance in our world today.

In my more than forty plus years of full time ministry, I have watched trust for the Bible's teaching on "wives submitting to husbands" crumble. But I have also observed a constant. Most every wife I've ever met wants to be able to *lean* on her husband. It is the way God made women. They don't want their husbands to push them over, dominate or lean on them. Nor do they want their husbands to be push overs themselves, or allow themselves to be dominated by their wives. But a woman wants to *lean on* the man she loves and respects.

And when I say lean, metaphorically, I don't mean leaning to the extent that she would fall over if he wasn't there for some reason, or leaning so heavily on him that he would topple over.

This is a mistake many women make as they approach marriage. They look for a husband on whom they can fully lean and cast all of their emotional weight upon. But that creates imbalance in the relationship, especially in a culture that encourages women to take charge. It's one of the reasons many husbands fall short in marriage. They weren't made by God to be a "*throw all your weight on me*" kind of support for their wives. God intended that men would be good leaning posts, not support columns or girders.

When I played football in high school, they taught offensive players when they get set on the scrimmage line in their bent over three point stances, to not place all of their weight on the single supportive arm. The coaches would come along and push on those arms and if the players toppled over, it was an indication they were putting too much weight on the supporting arm. A defensive player could simply swipe the arm and the offensive lineman would topple over and be overcome easily by his opponent. The one arm touching the ground was for balance not support.

The same idea can be used to describe a wife leaning on her husband. The wife leans; but if the husband were to move or fail in some way, the leaning wife would still stand. God made wives to lean and husbands were made to be someone the wife should be able to lean on.

This balance will create love, need, support, and a degree of dependency between the two; but not undue pressure. It allows for each to be as God made them. It allows the woman to be the valuable gift she was created by God to be for her husband. It allows for trust, respect and equality, and still clings to the instruction in Ephesians for how wives and husbands are to interrelate.

So what's a woman to do?

Wives, learn to *lean* on your husbands. Lean on them in ways that cause them to rely on their God-given abilities to guide a home. Lean on them so that they can be the strength you need. Lean on them to let them know you respect them. Lean on them to teach them how to be the stabilizers you need them to be. If you lean lovingly on your man, he won't let you fall.

3
Men

Now let's talk about *men*. I have two thoughts as I consider the issues between the sexes as they pertain to men.

First, one thing is certain; men in general don't know what a man should look like today. Should he be strong and confident before women; or tender and understanding? Should he be Mr. Man or Mr. Mom? Should he rule the house or clean the house? Should he bring home the bacon or cook the bacon?

It used to be that there were well defined lines dividing the roles of men and women. However, it is clear that those lines aren't nearly as certain as they were a half century ago. Some have concluded that our current culture has been shaped by the Woman's Liberation Movement of the 1920's, and has brought much confusion to men's minds. But regardless of where the confusion began, it is clear there is indeed a great deal of uncertainty about what a man should look like.

I would also say; men's minds aren't the only ones that are confused. Women are confused about what a real man should be as well. However, this confusion didn't start with the Woman's Liberation Movement of the late 1960's or any other similar event. The confusion began the moment sin entered the hearts of humans; and men's treatment of women from that point, and over the course of human history is proof enough of that.

Today many beer commercials will try to tell you that any man holding a beer in one hand and a girl wearing a bikini in the other is a real man. Some late night talk show hosts would like to communicate that a real man is a sexual idiot who is more enamored with the cheer leaders at half time than with the football game. Some images suggest that the real man is into sports, hunting, NASCAR and large muscles. Some say men work and women stay home and take care of the house. And some images say no; real men cook, clean and change diapers.

The reality is, all the uncertainty is the result of the fall. Sin entered the heart of mankind and as a result people in general have lost their grip on the reality that men and women are in fact equally made. Men don't know how to act around weaker vessels that are equal to them. And women don't know how to act in a culture with a media that has elevated them to being super-heroines, corporate executives, ninja champions and invincible covert spies. The result is; massive identity confusion. And yet, men, and our culture in general, continue to treat the weaker vessel as lesser, just as God said they would.

That leads me to my *second* thought on the matter. Since men don't know how to act around women, with sin driving them…they abuse. The point is; men don't know how to treat their wives, or women in general for that matter, and it has always been that way from earliest times. In every culture men have treated women poorly.

Christianity as described in the New Testament; is the first religious entity where we see treatment of women aim toward equality. Even cults that have splintered off of Christianity since its inception don't treat their women with as much respect as the New Testament instructs. It's amusing when I see the modern media try to suggest that Christianity is the cause of the poor treatment of women. They don't have a clue. Christianity is what set women free.

More than two thousand years ago Paul wrote some of the most astounding advice to men in the book of Ephesians on how to treat their wives with love and respect. Today it still stands as the best advice out there because it shows understanding of the equal creation of men and women while embracing their differences. In fact, any culture that does not embrace the Bible's take on this will wind up veering off into some other kind of ill-treatment of women like sexual exploitation, or gender misrepresentation, or labor oppression, or domination of some sort.

This is what Ephesians Chapter 5 says to husbands.

"Husbands, love your wives, just as Christ also loved the church and gave Himself for her, that He might sanctify and cleanse her with the washing of water by the Word, that He might present her to Himself a glorious church,

> *not having spot or wrinkle or any such thing, but that she should be holy and without blemish. So husbands ought to love their own wives as their own bodies; he who loves his wife loves himself. For no one ever hated his own flesh, but nourishes and cherishes it, just as the Lord does the church. For we are members of His body, of His flesh and of His bones."*
>
> Ephesians 5:25-30 (NKJV)

I want to address five messages these verses communicate that if husbands will heed, they won't just help their marriages to survive -- they will infuse them with the potential to thrive.

One - Sacrifice

The *first* is *sacrifice*. Now, I know I have already said that women have the more natural inclination toward self-sacrifice. That doesn't mean men don't know what it is. Nor does it mean they can't do it. It means women are more naturally inclined in this direction; while men must be convicted to love in this way.

The instruction you just read in Ephesians is to Christian men who have experienced inwardly the 'death of Christ' in their own hearts. It is the only way they could understand what it means to *"love their wives as Christ loved the church and gave Himself for it."*

So, Christian husbands know experientially the sacrifice of Christ. It was lived out in their hearts at conversion when they died to their old lives (as Christ died on the cross), and then was confirmed when they allowed His Spirit to enter their hearts. Therefore, the Spirit of God who is in them convicts Christian men concerning this sacrifice (John 16:8 NLT). Can women be convicted along these lines as well? Sure. It's just that Paul's instruction here on how to love matrimonially is to men.

Then he says that men will do this best when they allow Christ's sacrificial death, with the assistance of the Holy Spirit, to bring conviction to their hearts to love their wives in the same way Christ loved the world. So, Paul tells husbands to love their wives with the same kind of sacrificial love that nailed Christ to the cross and kept Him there until He died. Jesus' love was seen in a dying sacrifice. Husband's love for their wives will be seen in a living sacrifice that resembles metaphorically the death of Jesus.

When I eat a sandwich I have a peculiar habit. It probably stemmed from my childhood days when I was made by my mother to eat all the crusts of my bread. I never liked the crusts, yet, I was always made to eat them.

However, in the process of eating thousands of these crust-surrounded sandwiches over many years I learned something. The best part of the sandwich is the center. So, since I was required to eat all of every sandwich I was served, and since I truly believe it is wasteful to discard the crusts, I developed a habit of eating the crusts first and saving the best part for last. The good news is…the best has been saved until the end. The bad news is…the center of a sandwich after the crusts are gone is usually the equivalent of only about one bite.

My wife knows all of this and one day she tested me. She waited until I had consumed every trace of crust on the sandwich I was eating, and only the best bite was left. Then she said, "Can I have a bite?"

I wasn't alert to her evil plan to test my level of sacrificial love for her. So I found myself in a serious place of consternation. I looked at the last and luscious center bite and then back at her seemingly serious face and uttered "Oh alright". A more enthusiastic "sure" would have been a better response. But after all, it was the last and best bite.

Well I passed the test; and I was rewarded. She said, "Oh you can have it. I just wanted to see if you would sacrifice your precious last bite for me." So I gobbled it up before she could change her mind!

It's a silly little illustration of sacrifice. However, if men will be alert to making more significant and timely sacrifices for their wives with this principle in mind, rather than being selfish, or what this world defines as "manly," it will represent huge steps forward toward marriage prosperity.

For example, instead of going golfing, or hunting, or fishing; sacrifice and go shopping with your wife. And make these sacrifices as a regular routine. These kinds of sacrifices communicate to your wife that you love her sacrificially. A relationship filled with love and respect for each other is a much better reward than a day of golf. Don't worry men, you'll get your alone time if you sacrifice. But if you don't, you might not get your marriage back. The phrase Ephesians 5:25 uses is, *"Husbands, love your wives as Christ loved the church and gave (or sacrificed) himself for it."*

I find the best way for husbands to live this principle out is to develop a rhythm of sacrifice. By this I mean, develop practices that you can do regularly that communicate sacrifice to your wives.

For example; at some point I learned that my wife really valued it when I went shopping with her. So I began going shopping with her every time she went. It may seem like an insignificant thing, however, it communicates to her that I want to be with her. It's a rhythm of sacrifice I have developed.

Another is represented by a habit of conversation on our porch swing. I talk about this in more detail in a few sections so I won't elaborate here. Some husbands have developed a rhythm of serving their wives coffee in the morning. I advise every husband to discover what rhythms of sacrifice they can develop and live out with their wives that will communicate to their spouses that they love them with a love that is similar to the sacrificial love Christ demonstrated on the cross.

Two - Conversation

The *second* principle is *conversation*. The phrase "washing of water with the Word" in verse 28 is an indirect reference to talking.

I would like to bring you back to the little phrase in Genesis 3:16, *"Her desire shall be to her husband."* This statement also has to do with conversation. One of the top researched problems in women is low self-esteem. And, one of the top researched needs of women is conversation. Men should talk, and it is certainly helpful for them if they do. But for women it seems to be a need.

However, my experience is; men and their women don't talk. Walls are easily erected between spouses. One of the ways walls go up is if anger festers. Ephesians 4:26 advises to "never go to bed angry" because incubated anger builds walls. Some men are awkward with conversation. Some men are afraid of intimacy. Some men have things to hide; and there are other ways walls go up.

I will ask couples who have been married twenty years if they can tell me certain things about each other that they should have known in the first few weeks of their relationship and they can't. They can't because they never talk about anything deeper than *"What's for dinner?"* or *"Did you wash my underwear?"* This is a huge problem, because as conversation doesn't take place between spouses, trust unravels, the woman's self-esteem goes South, and coldness between a husband and his wife becomes more and more frigid. And with men who have a tendency to abuse, it can actually become dangerous for their ladies.

Women need to talk.

It astounds me when I consider the amount of conversation that can go on between two or more ladies in a room together with a lot of time on their hands. But, if studies are correct, it is necessary. And yet, women don't really need to talk with other women as much as they need and want to talk with their husbands. As this happens, it will build both of them up, raise the trust factor between them and significantly downgrade a wife's problems with low self-esteem.

Now with men it is different. As I said, men don't need to talk to their wives in order for them to feel good about themselves. Their self-esteem can be built up from their accomplishments and their professions; but not so with women. As the scripture says, *"Her desire shall be for her husband."* Her self-image is built up by her husband.

So, men, if you want to bring another level of calm to the issues between the sexes in your household, talk to your wife about more than just the weather, dinner and your underwear. Give her the respect of your attention and your interest in her.

But there is another angle to this idea of conversation. Low self-esteem is the result of no conversation. But high self-esteem is the result of much uplifting conversation. God wants all his children to reach their highest potential in life and in Him.

There are many men in our world with their own problems of low self-esteem; and some men have severe self-image issues. Woe to the woman who hooks up with one of these. However, they aren't easy to detect. Often, it isn't until couples are together several years that a wife discovers that she is married to a husband who has abusive and controlling tendencies that are an out-growth of his own low self-esteem.

These men can change, but only with influence from the transforming power of the Holy Spirit. Another book I have written called *Once Broken* will be able to help with that healing. However, until healing happens, these men keep their women down. They won't allow them freedom. Their wives can't have many friends, and they better tow the mark. These men exist in every level of society; the poor and the rich, the educated and the uneducated. They think if their wives aren't controlled they might outdo them, or leave them, which would increase their bad feelings about themselves.

My wife and I took a lady by the name of Gina (not her real name) to dinner one night. She had just gone through a difficult divorce. Her husband had been the kind of man who controlled her and kept her down. Yet, she was an extremely gifted and talented lady. A flurry of crashes in her husband's life finally caused her to realize her own life, and the rest of her family, would go under with him if she didn't get out. So Gina filed for divorce.

At the dinner, on a napkin, I had a thought and drew the picture of a small stick-figure woman standing next to a big stick-figure woman, but folded the napkin over so she could only see the small figure.

I showed her the smaller picture and said, "Gina, this lady is you when you were with your husband. You were beautiful, and an awesome lady. You were very capable and I felt you had the potential to do much in life and for the Lord." Then I opened the napkin up so she could see both of the figures standing next to each other. Then I said, "But Gina this is also you. I feel, now that you are away from him there is a much greater potential for you to become the bigger person that God has planned for your life."

She knew I was right. Every day of her married life she had felt the oppressive weight of her husband's dysfunction over her; keeping her down, holding her under his thumb, and imprisoning her under his control. She had already squandered many years under his reign of terror over her, and as she sat there she began to cry realizing she was now free to become. In my last contact with her which was many years later, she still kept that napkin in her Bible.

Men, as you ponder the responsibility of the wife and home you have been or will be given, remember; God wants you to understand you have the power to keep down and keep low the lives under your care. But you also have the power to enhance greatness in them. He expects you to help your wife become all that He has designed her to be. This can happen simply by conversing with her regularly and employing words of affirmation.

Three - Intimacy

The *third* area is *intimacy*. But you are going to be surprised at this one because at first glance it isn't what it seems. I am not talking about sex when I refer to intimacy. The secular world will tell you great sex is the cornerstone of a lasting marriage. It has some value. But if that is all a marriage has, believe me the relationship is doomed to crash.

In using the term intimacy I am talking about a greater degree or higher level of communication. And you will find that this discussion is the key to stopping wandering eyes in relationships and establishing singular devotion between spouses.

I do not believe in true love. I believe in puppy love, and first love, and tough love, and God's love. But I don't believe in true love. Hollywood would like to tell us that if we are able to find true love, it will insure that our marital or cohabitation relationships will last forever. And if a relationship doesn't last forever it must not have been true love. Frankly, I think it is a pretty naïve and uninformed perspective.

First, there are no definitions for true love. People just say you will know it when you find it. Really? It doesn't quite seem fair since most have never experienced anything like it their whole lives. If romantic relationships require true love in order for them to last forever, and most never find it, a whole lot of people are being ripped off in this life.

But second, most relationships who claim to have found true love don't last forever. They wind up falling prey to the same "break-up-itis" every other divorce experiences. And that is the primary reason I don't believe in it.

And third, successful marriages don't require true love. They require a commitment to work, a lot of work, hard work. And with hard work they can do more than last, they can flourish.

Let's get back to this idea of conversational intimacy. Intimacy for men *is* hard work. Sex is easy for men. Men do sex without thought, unfortunately, way too often. But for men to talk about intimate things is a grueling exercise. Yet, it is the kind of hard work that will solidify their relationship with their wives and keep both of them from having wandering eyes for others.

In verses 26 and 27 of Ephesians 5, communication is mentioned along-side of sanctifying, cleansing and Christ presenting a bride to Himself without spot or wrinkle; as well as the ideas of holiness and being without blemish. These may seem like random ideas to some, but they have a huge amount of relevance to each other, as well as a great amount of significance to the preservation of marriages and marital relationships.

The literal meaning of the word holy is "to set apart." Sanctify is from the same root word.

In the wilderness when God had Moses and the Israelites construct the first portable temple; He asked them to anoint it and all of the instruments within; such as candlesticks, bowls and furniture. They anointed these things with a special blend of holy anointing oil God had put together Himself. When these items were anointed they were deemed holy, sanctified, or "set apart" for God's use in worship.

Paul brings this same concept together with the idea of husbands communicating with their wives. He is trying to encourage husbands to have meaningful conversations with them that will not just cement their relationship together in intimacy; but with this intimacy they will "set their wives apart" for their husbands. This is intended to create singular devotion between them and ward off wandering eyes for other parties at the same time. It is as though these types of conversations act as a kind of anointing oil that sanctifies...that is, cements two people together.

When I talk about meaningful, tender and intimate conversations, I'm not referring to conversations about feelings and sex. I am talking about things that are important to both men and women; things like the future, dreams, daily struggles and frustrations, mutual hurts, the kids, spirituality, their jobs.

I don't quite know how this works, but when wives aren't given this kind of conversational affirmation they feel empty and unfulfilled. They feel like the sex they are asked to provide for their husbands is more like sexual abuse than it is mutual consent, and duty rather than pleasure. They feel like they are being used more than appreciated. Then, when someone of the opposite sex shows a wife any kind of affection, it has the allurement of romance and the feel of excitement. More so, with the husband, since the sex he has with his wife is just sex, he is also easily swayed by advances from other females. What you have as a result is clearly deception.

That is why Paul challenges men to talk tenderly, intimately and meaningfully with their wives because it has an ability to create single devotion between them and diminish the temptation to let their eyes wander in other directions. It feeds her soul, and then; it set's spouses apart for each other.

Several years ago friends gave us a porch swing. We hung it from our porch ceiling and it has become in no uncertain terms, the glue that has held our marriage together. Mornings on days off, evenings after dinner, other times when we have opportunity and sometimes when we don't; we gravitate to the swing to talk about anything and everything, tender things, hard things, intimate things, meaningful things. When we moved to another city we took it down and brought it with us to our new house and it served us in our marriage at our new location, and the next, and the next.

My advice is; find your porch swing. It may be a bench in a park, a boulder on a hillside, a pathway you may walk, or an overlook you may drive to, or the living room in your home. But whatever it is-- find it.

Four - The Golden Rule of Marriage

The *fourth* area is *The Golden Rule* as it relates to marriage. Most of us know what the Golden rule is. Jesus said, "Do to others as you would have others do to you" (Matthew 7:12). Well, a similar rule exists in marriage and is described in Ephesians 5:28 and 29.

Being a pastor and counselor I have encountered, especially in the last decade, a lot of people who cut themselves in order to diminish emotional pain. People who do this are experiencing great amounts of inner trauma. However, they have found that if they will inflict physical pain upon their flesh by cutting and drawing blood from their arm or wrist or some other area of their body, the shock of the wound will cause them to focus their minds off of their emotional trauma. It is, as you can imagine, a destructive coping mechanism because it will quickly cause the person who cuts to develop a mind-tilt so to speak, and begin to think physical pain fixes emotional pain. It is akin to drug addiction in that the drug habit also communicates that a substance high diminishes bad feelings. It does not, it only puts them off; as does cutting.

But we think differently about cutters than we do addicts. We tend to think cutters have crossed a line of reality, and it is probably correct. They can get their thinking straight again. But until they do they are 'off' in their thinking with regards to this particular issue.

By the way, this is not a new practice. The Bible tells of a man who was doing the same thing in in Jesus' day (Mark 5:5). And the Old Testament talks about people cutting themselves in idol worship.

Why all this psychological talk about cutters? Well, Ephesians 5:28-29 actually alludes to the example of cutters. It says, "No one hates his flesh, but nourishes it and cherishes it." The suggestion is people shouldn't harm themselves…instead, they take care of themselves.

Here is what Paul is saying: Since marriage makes husbands and wives *one* by reason of the union of their marriage; if a husband physically, mentally, emotionally or verbally harms his wife, he is actually harming himself. Since harming oneself is not a normal practice, Paul is suggesting that if a husband *is* normal, he won't harm his wife in any way because it is the same as harming himself.

On the positive side of this point, if a man is wise he will do whatever he can to lift up, build up and talk up his wife; both to her and to others and even to himself, because when he does he is taking care of himself because she is one with him.

Verse 29 also gives a two-fold methodology to accomplishing this rule. It uses the words *nourish* and *cherish* and says in effect, "As Jesus nourished and cherished His church, so should husbands nourish and cherish their wives." In other words it is saying, *"This is how you do it—you do it like Jesus nourished and cherished His church."*

Nourish means to feed. Does that mean Husbands are to spoon feed their wives food, or cook the meals, or go to chef's school? No! They are to feed them emotionally, spiritually, socially, verbally and communally.

As a rule, women are more conversational than men. There are exceptions to this, but for the most part it is true. But emotional, spiritual and verbal communication doesn't necessarily require talking.

Many men will talk to their wives but be a million miles away. The kind of nourishing this scripture is talking about simply requires men to be present when they are with their wives. Don't just be with your wife when you are with her; actually be present when you are with her. Don't be on the golf course, or thinking about the football game, or negotiating a business contract with a customer when you are with your wife. Feed her need for your attention. Men nourish their wives when they give their minds, bodies, hearts and souls to their spouses. And when they do, life-giving conversation will happen as well.

Cherish means to warm or foster. It speaks of tenderness and gentle encouragement.

Men can be rough and careless at times. They punch each other, chest bump, push each other down and wrestle with one another just for fun; and no bruises occur. But if men were to treat women in the same way, their ladies would get bruises all over their bodies.

I wonder if God made women that way just so men would have a barometer with which to judge how carefully they should treat their wives. But I'm not just talking about physical treatment. I'm also talking about communication.

Peter doesn't call women the weaker vessel just because women in general can't press as much weight as men or run as fast (I Peter 3:7). They are also called the weaker vessel because they are more sensitive emotionally. It's why when challenged or pressed they cry so easily. For men to cherish their wives is to be sensitive to their emotional makeups; and for men to be sensitive in this way is to love them. If they do, their wives will love them and be endeared to them in return.

These two words describe how husbands are to treat their wives because as they nourish and cherish them in this way, they are treating themselves this way.

It's the golden rule of marriage and the massage therapy of matrimony. What man wouldn't want a massage from his wife? I would take one from my wife at just about any time she would be willing to give it. Do to your wives as you would have them do to you. Massage them emotionally.

Five - Triple Spirituality

The *fifth* challenge from Ephesians 5 that will help marriages thrive is *spirituality*. Notice verse 30 says, *"We are members of His body, of His flesh and of His bones."* Of all the points in these verses, this one has rescued my marriage more than any other, multiple times over.

A "born of the Spirit" relationship with God is the only one the Bible endorses. John 3:5 says without it one cannot enter the kingdom of God. When we genuinely come to Christ, His Holy Spirit enters our bodies which actually become His temple (1Corinthians 6:19). God's Spirit in us is there for many purposes, one of which is to convict us of sin and lead us into righteous living (John 16:8, 13).

If it weren't for God's Spirit in me leading and guiding me in this way, I would have fallen many times. There have been many lies I have *not* told because His Spirit spoke louder to me than my own desires. There have been many things I have *not* stolen because God's Spirit spoke up just in time. There have been many, many words I have *not* spoken because I was checked by the Holy Spirit in me. There have been many sins I *did not* commit because the Holy Spirit inside of me shouted His advice to me just as I was about ready to make the wrong choice.

One of the most potentially volatile areas of life is marriage—dare I say…*the* most volatile. I can't count the number of times the Holy Spirit has said to me just as I was about ready to speak an offensive remark to my wife; *Don't say that.* Or, *you better wait before you tell her that.* Or, *that wouldn't be a very wise response, better keep it to yourself.* Or, *I wouldn't call her that name you are thinking of right now,* or *make that suggestion,* or *do what you are planning.* Without this help from the Lord, I don't think my marriage would have survived. Maybe you are smarter than me and you can do it on your own. But I need God's help.

Before I knew the Lord I had some common sense and some restraint. But it just wasn't enough, and I had no knowledge of God's Word or His wisdom. So I relied on the small amount of wisdom I possessed which was very limited. However, even that small amount of wisdom was tainted with sin which shaped every decision I made and the voice of *my* wisdom got me into trouble many times. Since the goal of sin is to destroy me and everything in my life, including my marriage and family; that wasn't a very good voice to listen to. Fortunately, Christ came into my life before it was too late; and just in time to offer life-giving direction to the vital areas of my life, the greatest of which was my marriage.

The difficult part about applying this principle to marriage is: marriage is a highly emotionally charged relationship. When we become one mentally, emotionally and physically, in addition to offering our undivided loyalty to our spouse; it infuses the relationship with energy but more than that, it infuses the relationship with explosive potential for good or bad. The good explosions are fine. But the bad can be really bad.

I have counseled couples that were so volatile they emitted violent eruption after violent eruption right in front of me. One can only imagine how destructive their communication must have been toward each other when I was not around to curtail the violence.

When lines are crossed in communication it seems all rules are off. And when this happens, it is immensely difficult for a Christian to hear the voice of the Holy Spirit. It's possible but not easy. But God is there just the same and is trying to get through to us in an effort to help us in our relationship. We just need to learn to listen.

The scripture here in verse 30 suggests that a successful marriage isn't one with two people; instead, it has three partners. Those three are her, him and Jesus. And this is the function of each; Jesus leading her, and Jesus leading him; him hearing Jesus and her hearing Jesus; and then him obeying Jesus and her obeying Jesus. I call it <u>triple spirituality</u>, and it must be present in a marriage if it is to, not just survive, but thrive!

4

Mutual Submission

It is in the area of mutual submission where marriage can be a 50-50 proposition. Everywhere else, either men's or women's traits must be considered. But mutual submission levels the playing field.

The first verse in the Ephesians' marriage passage, verse 21, is all about submission, but not from just the wife.

> *"And further, submit to one another out of reverence for Christ."*
>
> Ephesians 5:12 NLT

It is calling for mutual submission from both toward each other. In other words, both marriage partners are to be about the objective of submitting to one another. The context suggests that the environment of marriages is supposed to be submission from each, to each, not as some have errantly assumed, that wives submit and men rule. No! The environment of marriages that survive, and even those that thrive, must have two hearts that are submitted to each other.

What is submission?

The dictionary suggests that it is the act of yielding to a superior authority or person. Biblical submission inserts a small element that changes the whole complexion of the definition. It calls for a submitted heart in each spouse for each other.

The dictionary's definition of submission will work if one yields with a resistant heart. Like one saying, "*I'll do what he says because if I don't I might lose my job.*" It represents an <u>act of submission but not a heart of submission</u>.

Submission isn't something we do with gritted teeth. Saying something like…*I don't like it. I don't agree with it. I think you are completely wrong. But I will bite my tongue and give in.* That isn't submission. That's passive defiance and with this kind of submission it is only a matter of time before there is trouble.

Submission in the Bible is different.

Submission in scripture can be considered a companion trait to humility. Humble people have submissive hearts. Submitting to someone in the way the Bible describes is the kind of thing that cannot be done unless one is humble. It is hard for someone to submit in the way God's Word describes if that one is defiant. In fact, it is impossible.

True submission calls for a submissive heart. One is so devoted to the other; both hearts are yielded to each other. It's like a true and unified team. No one takes a posture of being in charge over the other. They work their situations out together.

What does this kind of submission look like in a marriage? Below are five areas where mutual submission will make for marriages that thrive.

Listen

Listening is one of the hardest things for people to do…especially men. What kinds of responses represent non-listening; interruptions, threatened reactions, impatience, casual body language, boredom and falling asleep? I'm sure you have encountered some if not all of these with different people in different situations. Listening is hard.

However, a submitted heart in a relationship appreciates things the other has to say because the person expressing those things is valued. If spouses have submitted hearts for the other, they will listen and understand.

In our home from time to time one of us will say that there are 'some things we need to talk about'. Both my wife and I know what that means. It means one is going to tell the other about something or some things the other has said or done that will be critical in nature.

In many homes, when this happens, spouses run for the hills. This response shouts "I don't want to hear it." Usually, this represents an even deeper feeling of insecurity. We don't want to be challenged, or corrected, or told we are wrong, or made to feel to blame for whatever we may have done. But we shouldn't think of these times as threatening. We should think of these times as trouble-shooting times, and we should be secure enough to sit down and discuss how we will resolve the trouble this time and negotiate it the next time.

Recently I watched the story of John Gotti, starring Al Pachino. It claimed to be the true expression of what happened to this iconic union figure, though they said there were still some uncertainties in the story. I was taken with the absolute childish attitude that this bigger than life man had about not wanting to talk to a certain person all because of his pride. He didn't want to hear it, or talk about it, or even be in the same room with the man. His ego was his downfall. This overpowering man was so adolescent in his behavior, it is what got him killed.

I see many spouses, especially men, but women too, who are afraid to hear it. They can't talk about things because their pride won't let it in. And many, if they are able to sit in a room and have a conversation with their spouse about whatever issue may need to be addressed, they leave determining, "I'll do what I want."

There are two reasons my wife and I don't go into avoidance mode and run for the hills as many do. We endeavor to come together and listen. First, we value each other. Second, we value the relationship. It may be a tough few minutes but we know we must face it if we are going to get over the hump that has been placed before us. We might disagree but we resolve to listen and understand the perspective of the other to ensure that the relationship can go on without the encumbrance of mistrust.

I didn't say listening was easy, and I didn't say it was fun. But if the marriage relationship <u>is to be fun</u>, we have to address the not-so-fun elements as well.

Not listening when your wife says to take out the garbage doesn't count. That's OK. Don't tell her I said that.

Release

Every marriage encounters issues that become sticking points in the relationship.

For example: A husband decides he wants a dog for the kids; but the wife didn't grow up with dogs so she isn't comfortable having them in the house and feels they are unsanitary. Thus, we have a stalemate. Each one feels he or she is right and things come to a standstill. I've seen marriages split up over lesser issues. So . . . let it go.

This was a real issue in mine and my wife's relationship. She 'let it go' and interestingly she fell in love with the dog and I became weary with having one. The issue is never as important as the relationship, the family, the children's lives and their futures. Who got their way, who won, and who gained leverage for future power struggles; are all miniscule victories compared to maintaining the relationship and the family. Actually, they aren't victories at all. They are losses for each, with heavy casualties. Ninety-nine percent of the issues that people, for pride, hang on to are never as important as the relationship.

If needs be, let it go one hundred times without the other following suit. Don't say, "Hey, I let it go last time. It's your turn this time." It's not something where we take turns letting go so spouses can save face. That's just another way pride can wedge its way into the relationship.

When posed with the option, let it go as many times as needs be before the other decides to let it go.

Many marriages become competitions between the two where each keeps score by subconsciously marking victories for one or the other. "You got your way last time so I get mine this time."

However, I think marriages should have three sides; the man, the woman and the relationship. Sometimes the man wins and gets a mark, and sometimes the woman wins and gets a mark. But the marriage where THE RELATIONSHIP has an overwhelming amount of winning marks is the relationship that will remain alive and ultimately thrive.

In Matthew 18:21-22, Peter asked Jesus if he should 'let it go' 7 times. Jesus responded to Peter's question, "Let it go (or forgive) 7 x 70 times," equaling 490 times. If Peter had specified that he was talking about marriage, the Savior may have answered 7 x 7,000,000 times.

Let it go.

Forgiveness

Speaking about forgiveness, offences happen in marriages. Offenses happen because all people, therefore all spouses, are sinners. Wrong words are spoken. Promises are broken. Tempers flare. Mistakes are made. People are unthoughtful. As a result, walls go up, mistrust mounts and voila; in millions of marriages there is bitter un-forgiveness.

I don't know how many times I've heard over the years from church members and clients, "I could never forgive him (or her) for that." The norm for non-forgiveness is an incubation of resentment over months and sometime years that grows and finally develops into an irreconcilable relationship.

I will be the first to admit that I am capable of harboring un-forgiveness. I can hold onto offences with the best of them, and I will acknowledge that it is truly difficult for me to muster forgiveness for people who have wronged me. So I am acquainted with the difficulty of forgiving.

Yet, in a marriage, forgiveness is required if it is to keep going—because offences happen. Our sinful nature will see to that. To enter marriage with naïve presuppositions that forgiveness will never need to be granted because no forgivable situations will ever arise, is truly blind.

Then, once two people are in the marriage and one partner refuses to forgive, suggests the same naivete. Sometimes this unawareness causes he or she to believe that there are better people who do nothing offensive enough to mandate forgiveness; that there are more perfect people who will never do anything as dastardly as the spouse that offended them. So they are tempted to find another rather than forgive.

This just isn't true. There are no people who are less likely to do un-forgivable things because we are all equally sinful and fail with regularity and will require forgiveness in order to keep the relationship going. These people will just discover the need to forgive in the next relationship, and at some point, they will need to be the recipient of forgiveness.

There are very few scenarios where offenses are too great to forgive. In every church I have pastored there were couples who had been unfaithful to their spouses and the cheating spouse was forgiven, some more than once.

While I don't want to suggest that forgiveness in marriages is only about affairs, this kind of offense is just about as severe as it gets. If spouses can forgive this offense, certainly the lesser offenses that divide couples can be forgiven. And for your information, God considers affairs or any of the other typical offenses in marriage to be lesser than the spiritual debt he forgives in any person's life.

In Matthew 18:23-33, Jesus tells a parable that concludes with the implied lesson… *because we have been forgiven the greatest debt of all (our sinfulness) we should be able to forgive the lesser offenses that are dealt to us (like those that arise in marriage).*

Spouses – (specifically those who name Jesus as Lord), He has forgiven you the greatest debt that could ever have been accumulated in anyone's life; a mountain sized debt of sinfulness, or in the parable, a debt represented by millions of dollars. Never could you have eliminated a debt such as this from your life outside of the forgiveness of Christ.

The parable tells us that every sin done to us is infinitely lesser than this mountain of sinfulness piled up in our lives. Since God for Christ's sake has forgiven us for our enormous debt of sinfulness, he expects us to forgive others for the lesser sins they have done to us, because in comparison they are infinitesimal. They may seem big, but as they compare to forgiveness that offers eternal life and saving us from the fires of hell, they are minuscule.

Spouses, we can and we must forgive.

I'm Sorry

Many of the offenses suggested above develop into issues that are larger than life because we don't deal with them early on. Sometimes we even imagine betrayal or wrong intentions and we harbor them in our hearts, let them fester, and then grow into problems they never needed to grow into.

At the risk of oversimplifying, why don't we just say 'I'm sorry' before a question develops into an issue, and then into a problem, and then into a crisis. Speaking the phrase 'I'm sorry' requires hearts of submission.

'I'm sorry' for some, are the hardest two words to string together in any language. Pride grips our minds, then our hearts, then our jaws, then our tongues, then nothing comes out; or if it does, it comes out wrong permitting pride to slip back in.

I once saw a man come into the waiting area outside my office. I couldn't see him very well but could see him well enough to tell that he was extremely unsettled. He sat nervously for some time then rose and began to pace. He seemed to be in some kind of inner battle. Then he sat again, and paced again at least two more times until he finally worked up the nerve to come over to my door and knock.

After I let him in he sat nervously down and fidgeted while I settled myself in a chair across from

I Do, Do You?

him. I asked him what was on his mind. Instead of answering he seemed to be fighting some kind other of inner battle. He would almost speak; then he would back off. This second battle went on for at least a minute.

Finally he said through what appeared to be restrained jaws and lips, "I'm sorry."

His 'sorry' was for thinking something about me he was feeling guilty for and something I had no idea he felt.

But when he said it he relaxed, peace came over him and me, since I was extremely concerned about what he might say or do.

Another time, I said the same two magic words to a player in a basketball group that played pickup games in a few mornings a week at a gym in my area. I could tell he was getting noticeably irritated with me over the weeks. Yet, I had no idea what I had done to bother him. But I was certain he was having a problem with me.

I entertained the notion of never going back. That was how I was going to deal with it until God spoke to me.

I met him on the way into the gym the next time we were to play, pulled him aside and said, "I'm sorry." I didn't know what I had done so I didn't know what I needed to say I was sorry for. But I knew, if nothing else, I had perpetuated the issue by not confronting it sooner; so that was what my 'sorry' was for I guess.

When I voiced the two amazing words, his suspicious, ready to retaliate countenance softened. We made up and there was never a problem again.

A truly intended, gently worded 'I'm sorry' is difficult to speak but is magical in the marriage environment. These two words melt icy hearts and prohibit the budding of resentment before it can blossom into relationship damaging mistrust.

Be quick to say 'I'm sorry.'

Rightness

Human nature, or maybe more accurately the sinful nature, is to be right. So natural is this human nature of ours, it spills over into marriage. Spouses, almost with obsession, desire to be right. It is akin to whatever prompted Eve to want to be like God, knowing good and evil. She wanted power.

The drive to be right in marriages escalates arguments. It exaggerates issues. It prolongs fights. It blinds people to the foolishness of their opinions. It drives wedges between spouses. It compels individuals to rally support with other family members and friends against their mates. It causes spouses to sleep in different bedrooms. It causes separations. It perpetuates divorce.

If you have an issue with your spouse, are you sure it isn't just a power-issue?

There was a couple in one of the churches I pastored that loved teaching Sunday school to kids. However, they would always seem to come up with the wackiest ideas for their classes. In fact, I once heard an idea of theirs after the fact and I said to the person who told me about it, "No, they really didn't do that did they? It couldn't have worked. I need to tell them they should never do that again."

But the person stopped me and said, "No, don't do that. It was a smashing success. The kids loved it and they love these teachers more than any other."

I don't remember what their idea was, but I learned a lesson that day. Often, the right thing to do is secondary to who is doing it. I thought it was wrong and it wouldn't work. They thought it was right and made it work.

I have come to realize the same is true in marriage. Often there aren't right and wrong ideas. There are two right ideas from the perspective of the different ones offering their opinions.

So don't be headstrong about being right and your spouse being wrong. Both may be right. But have the courage and a heart that is humble enough to let your mate be right.

But the real issue about who is right in a marriage is usually a pride thing where neither refuses to give in. This is where submissive hearts need to prevail, where one says, "Ok Dear, I don't know if you are right or not. But let's try it your way."

Exclamation Point!

The issues of the sexes do not need to be fiercely addressed. They can be quite tame if we learn how to incorporate the five marriage messages to men of Ephesians 5, the four principles posed to women, and the common divisive sticking points concerning mutual submission.

In Matthew 24:38 it says, *"In the last days people will be marrying and giving in marriage."* Some have asked... "What does that mean?" I say, "What you see happening right now is what that means."

Some versions interpret this scripture to mean that people will just be going about their routines, getting married with no care for the future. I would theorize that it means more.

What with all the divorce in our world today, and couples living together outside of the marriage commitment, and remarriages, and adultery, and same sex marriages, and open marriages, and free marriages, and spouse swapping marriages; I think what Jesus called it means all of this.

I believe this because the issue then wasn't what they were doing. The issue was they were doing it because they didn't care that it may result in their doom. Today, a similar nonchalant attitude about peoples' fate exists, and it is seen in the different ways that people approach the subject of marriage.

Needless to say, the value system for marriage has crumbled. Sacredness in marriage has become a value of the past. Even Christian couples wanting to marry, who claim to possess the value of "forever-ness" in marriage, in conjunction with their devotion to the Savior; don't realize that our culture has weakened this value in their hearts. And couples won't know it until a crisis in their marriage brings it to light.

I have encountered many couples who felt their Christian status, would, in it-self, insulate their relationship against the contemporary onslaughts of marriage. They feel the fact that both are Christians will insure marriage success. But that is just another myth.

I Do, Do You?

Marriage is our world's last great hope for happiness in this life, as long as it is done in Christ. But it has been riddled with so many cultural bullets that it is a weakened hope at best. And that is all the more reason that couples wanting to capture the happiness marriage promises must do it God's way, following His commands, and observing His instructions.

Marriage is God's invention. It works best when His blueprint for its success is followed. The principles in this book are biblically sound. They aren't exhaustive. They don't cover every bit of the Bible's instruction about marriage. However, if couples desire to have a successful marriage, a marriage that is filled with happiness, surrounded with contentment, infused with love and brimming with life; they must follow the directives God gives here in Ephesians Five.

So the question to couples becomes…Do you solemnly swear to do marriage God's way; obeying His commands about marriage, following His guidelines and trusting His instructions in your marriage relationship with your spouse? Do you?

I_____!   I_____!
    Husband   Wife

5
Questions for Study – Building Marital DNA

All parts of this book should be read by both the man and the woman. However, some questions are gender-specific and should only be answered by the man or the woman. These questions are identified in the different sections. But both should know what is being asked of the other.

There is a myth that happens in marriage; maybe it is more of a wrong assumption. The assumption is: If a spouse decides on his or her own to do something loving for his or her partner, then it is sincere. If he or she is told about something to do, or reads about something and then does it, it is an insincere gesture and should not be received.

I don't know where this idea came from, but it is one of the most ridiculous assumptions I have ever heard. But people assume it just the same.

There are so many unknown ideas in the Bible about how to make marriage work better, the only way to glean them would be to read and discover them. For a spouse to expect her partner to know them or think of them on his or her own would be unrealistic.

Furthermore, love is not seen in knowing, because many know a lot of things to do but never act on them. Love is seen in doing something, whether known, discovered, learned <u>or</u> told.

This is why I am asking both spouses to read and discover what is being said to the other. The accountability will be good for each, as well as give opportunity to help each with clarity on what is preferred.

Questions for Men and Women

The Basis for Marriage Success

1. After reading this book, husband, now what is your idea of the perfect wife? List your descriptions. Wife: after reading this book, what is your idea of the perfect husband?
List your descriptions.

2. Which of the above descriptions do you think Jesus and God's Word would agree with? Why?

3. Re-read Genesis 3:16. Wife, what do you think "your desire shall be for your husband" means? Husband, what do you think "he shall rule over you" means?

4. Do you feel men and women are equal? In what ways? In what ways not?

5. Each of you: what do you feel are the three most difficult things about dealing with the opposite sex? Why?

Women – For women only to answer:

1. Describe with examples what selfless love would be for a wife.

2. What do you think "weaker vessel" might mean?

3. What would you do if you felt your husband mis-treated you?

4. How do you feel about the use of the phrase "lean on" rather than the word submit when it comes to the husband/wife relationship?

5. Are you approaching marriage with the idea that you need, or you are counting on, your husband being a strong man to lean on?

What's a Woman to Do? – For women only to answer

1. Are you as a wife willing to implement "selfless love" in your marriage? In what ways have you already seen yourself living this role out? In what ways can you see yourself living this out in the future?

2. How will you live out your equality with your husband? Before your husband?

3. Do you know the difference between 'needing to express emotions' and 'neediness in the expression of emotions'? Describe the difference.

4. How will you help your husband to express his emotions?

5. How will you utilize your discernment capabilities (or reasonableness) in your marriage so that it doesn't cause your husband to feel dominated or controlled?

6. Do you feel you want your husband to be someone you can lean on? Describe in what ways.

Men – For men only to answer

1. How would you describe what a real man looks like morally and spiritually?

2. Do you have confusion in your mind about what a "real man" should look like? Describe your confusion.

3. How would you describe what your treatment of your wife will look like after reading this book?

4. Have you noticed anything in you that feels like it could turn into abuse toward your wife? What? (It should be noted that the sin in all men will possess these tendencies. Men's ability to say no is the way men overcome).

One – Sacrifice

1. Describe what you think a "living sacrifice" for your wife might be.

2. What kinds of things will you be ready to sacrifice for your wife?

3. What will your rhythm of sacrifice look like?

Two – Conversation

1. Describe your talking quotient by rating it on a continuum from 1 to 10…10 being "talks a lot." What will you do to increase your talking quotient with your wife?

2. Will you obey Ephesians 4:26… "never go to bed angry"? What do you think it will take to obey this rule?

3. What kind of schedule will you set to talk with your wife?

4. Do you feel you are responsible for the level of self-esteem your wife has? Why or why not?

5. How would you describe your own level of self-esteem?

6. How will you help your wife to become all that God has made her to be?

Three – Intimacy

1. What kinds of subjects do you think would be in a meaningful conversation?

2. What kinds of things do real men talk about?

3. How will you feed your wife's soul?

Four – The Golden Rule of Marriage

1. Describe what you think "the two become one" in marriage means.

2. Have you ever "put down" your wife/fiancé in front of others? How was that received?

3. Have you ever built up your wife/fiancé in front of others? What did you say? How was that received?

4. What would you need to change in order to treat your wife gently?

5. What would you do to cherish your wife?

Five – Triple Spiritually

1. Do you have a "born of the Spirit" relationship with the Lord? Describe what it means to you.

2. If you do, what does God's voice to you sound like when sin of any kind is before you? What does His voice sound like after you have erred and committed sin?

3. Describe a time when God's Spirit stopped you from saying or doing the wrong thing where your wife/fiancé is concerned.

4. Describe a time when you failed to listen to the Spirit concerning your wife/fiancé.

5. Describe what it means to you to have Jesus be the third member of your marriage union.

Mutual Submission – For both Men and Women to Answer

Listen

1. Do you find it hard to listen? Why? Why not?

2. Describe what you think 'listening between the lines' means.

3. Are you able to listen to what your spouse is saying between the lines? Discuss each other's ability to do this.

4. Explain what you think it means to listen without offering solutions.

5. Discuss how 'listening without offering solutions' may be a good thing.

Release

1. Discuss your ease or difficulty with letting things go.

2. Make two lists.
   - One of the things that are easy to let go of
   - One of things that are hard to let go of

   Discuss how you might be able to let the hard things go.

Forgiveness

1. Discuss the different ways pride is connected to un-forgiveness.

2. Discuss the different ways anger is related to un-forgiveness.

3. Discuss things you have forgiven in others in the past.

4. Could you forgive your spouse if he or she had an affair? Why? Why not?

5. Discuss the biblical concept from Matthew 18: 23-35; since Christ has forgiven us for our enormous debt of sinfulness, He expects us to forgive others for lesser offenses.

   List what some lesser offenses might be.

I'm Sorry

1. Discuss how saying 'I'm sorry' is related to humility.

2. Discuss how the two words 'I'm sorry' could be the most important words in your marriage relationship.

3. Why is it so hard for people to say, 'I'm sorry'?

4. Describe a time you went through the 'I'm sorry battle'?

5. When is the best time to say 'I'm sorry'?

Rightness

1. What is behind the desire in people, especially spouses, to be right?

2. Discuss the idea that 'the relationship is more important than being right'. Talk about some examples where this is true.

3. Which is better, to be right and divorced, or to be wrong and still married? Why might this be obvious. Discuss why this might not be obvious.

About the Author

Chris Schimel has a Master of Divinity degree and has been a pastor for more than four decades in churches from New York to California. He is the founder of Touch One Ministries and currently pastors a church in the Youngstown, Ohio area. He and his wife Shirley have two grown sons, Jeff and Joel.

Contacting the Author

chrisjschimel.com
chrisjschimel@gmail.com

I Do, Do You? is a companion book to Chris's book
Murder in the Church.
To acquire *Murder in the Church,* go to the book
page on Chris's website (listed above).

www.ingramcontent.com/pod-product-compliance
Lightning Source LLC
LaVergne TN
LVHW011736060526
838200LV00051B/3199